ECHOES FROM A FAR SHORE

David Hodges

B~ David Hodges

Echoes from a Far Shore

© David Hodges 2009

ISBN 0953322297
Acknowledgements
Spirituality, Religious life Review
and **The Merton Journal**
in which some of these poems first appeared

Published by The Abbey, Caldey Island,
Tenby, Pembs. SA70 7UH, Wales, G.B.

Echoes from a Far Shore:
John at Patmos

The deep green harbour
and the light-flooded sky
enter the blackness
of the cave's surround.
Here, from my exile,
rising I survey
the far horizon, the sun,
the endless sea and sky.

His love was boundless,
his wisdom far beyond
what I have written,
or could seek to understand.
His voice, his piercing gaze—
memories fade
like footprints in the sand.

I walked with him in love.
But prayer is all I have now,
no human consolation.
If God is love,
then I am tested sore.
All I have are
echoes from a far shore.

Nothing Can Prepare Us....

Nothing can prepare us,
not the crescent moon and stars,
not the hush and stillness,
nor the coolness of the breeze,
not the liturgy of birds
nor their interlacing flight,
not the currents playing
in the rippled sea,
not the first brightening
on the hilltops round the bay....
No, nothing can prepare us
for its suddenness,
its newness, the revelation
of its splendour....
for the white-hot fire of His love,
for the rising of the Son.

In Memory's Cave

In the darkest night,
along the blackest shore,
the silver moon slips
into memory's cave.
And limpid eyes,
and angel's silver wings,
shine through my dreams.

On Beauty

There goes Beauty,
naked Beauty,
dancing, dancing,
pirouetting,
free as air,
spreading garlands
and embracing
all that's good and true,
all that's pure
and penetrated
by God's heavenly light.
Eternal splendour,
dancing, dancing, dancing;
naked Beauty
playing in us,
love unfolding,
taking form,
bursting, budding,
fragrant,
catching breath,
transfigured in this space,
expressing something
of God's glory,
somehow mirrored
in us.

She Walks in Beauty

*'She walks in beauty, like
the night..'*
                    Byron

Lustrous beauty
circling bright,
with new, clear shafts
of silver light,
gliding through
the shadows of the night.
How brilliant is
the sweep of stars
that sparkle in her train!—
her veil the brightest
in the heavens.
Tuned to the music
of the spheres,
her song, her beauty
all express
her one, eternal 'yes'.
Reflected glory
of her Sun,
hers of right,
receptive of
his all-embracing light.

Winter Rosebud

Little Rosebud,
born out of time,
festive
in sparkling rime,
red and crystal
in the sun.

Then, every day
sporting a different
snow hat,
revealing in your
filmy coat,
showy in your
frosty jewels,
bravely opening
petals.

Now bent double
under weight of snow,
a different, near death
kind of look,
your colour
and plump fullness
gone, still
red at the edges.

Summer Watering

Rhubarb curls and flaps its ears,
gurgles with pleasure.
Parsley is frisky like a lamb,
while sage shrinks like a young child
in a shower.
Chives sound grateful,
firm up and squeak;
fennel sucks in delight.
Dill shines brightly like a cobweb,
while coriander just looks drowned.
Rosemary flexes its muscles,
giving off its sweet odour.
Weeds frown and nettles scowl,
as roses glisten, foxgloves dance
and evening primrose opens in a smile.
Hosed down and dripping,
the garden is visibly glad.

Bubble Netting

They did it for us
passing through Juno
on our celebration cruise.
First we saw the ocean bubbling,
then, half out of water,
coming up for air,
six huge humpback whales
bursting like missiles through the water,
poised, then disappearing
to continue their communal feed.
Diving deep
and breathing out together
to create a bubble net,
to catch their midday meal of krill;
then soaring to the surface,
hoovering up like factory ships,
open-mouthed
and with loud, excited cries.
Once in a lifetime sighting,
holding us rapt, full of wonder
at their synchronised swim
and agape meal.

From the Giant's Chair*

The red sun, slung
between two peaks,
we see reflected in the deep
and icy lake beneath.
Climbing sharp and steep,
from shadows cold and dark we meet
the frost-fire glare
from the Giant's chair.

Then later from the top is seen
his kingdom red and green,
from Cardigan to Brecon,
from Snowdon to the Borders.
And looking bravely down beneath,
the height and distance pull the soul,
until the peace is rudely broken
by Jaguar strike planes snaking
through his lair below.

*Cadair Idris, chair of the Giant Idris,
a mountain in North Wales

A Friday Afternoon in August

Hot and sultry,
no breath of air,
two full rows
of fragrant lavender—
all dancing butterflies,
bright insects, moths and bees.
Entranced I watch
a Walt Disney cartoon
against a shock of blue.

Entering the Abbey church
from the garden door,
two full rows in choir.
At the bell for None,
in angel tones
the psalm intoned.
Entering the sacred text:
'Brothers living in unity...
like precious oil...running down'.

Grace comes
light as moth wings,
time suspended,
journeying within.
Pure presence,
embraced in the One,
forgetting self,
embraced
in everyone.

My Inner Bird of Song

In the dim and darkened Church,
cold before the day breaks,
I struggle with the note
that breaks the silence of the night.
My faltering voice
fires into life,
like a trapped bird
that takes to flight
and cannot find the light;
that fights and fights
to find the light,
and when it finds the open door
to freedom soars.
The antiphon was never purer sung,
my inner bird of song.

The Old Priory

My house will be called
a house of prayer
for all peoples
Isaiah 56.7

A sanctuary filled with prayer
in every space, from cobbled floor
to barrel-vaulted roof.
Requests for prayer,
on scraps of card and paper,
left stacked on altar and piscina,
on every stand and ledge
and frame and alcove,
on hooks and nails,
in crevices in walls.
The candle-stand aflame
before the Virgin and her Child.
To God, I love you…
For all my loved ones,
keep them safe…
For grandad, Eve and baby Jane,
look after Tommy in heaven…
Only say the word,
help my nephew John
wake up from his coma…
Forgive me, look after
those I love…
Please look after my little brother,
may he rest in peace.
Love, Elli…
Stop all fighting in the world,
may there be peace…
Send every joy and blessing…

Keep me on the right path...
Thank you for your many gifts
for everyone I love,
for helping me off drugs,
thank you for being there for me...
Sleep tight, Mum and Dad,
thinking of you always, Tracey...
Put everything right again,
help get us back together...
Watch over all,
for those in any need...
For my grandad
with a leaky heart,
he has always believed in me...
Look after Karen,
let her stay free of cancer. Mum...
Forgive a doubter of his sins,
may I get to see my daughter...
Please help my Dad
to find someone and be happy
as my Mum is,
I love them both so much...
Watch over your world,
Holy Spirit guide us...
Bless our marriage...
I love and miss you every day...
Father, your will be done,
may my scan be clear...
Thank you for all the beauty
in this world...
Send your healing love...
Jesus, I lift them up to you,
I place them in your hands,
all those who have left their prayers
here on this Island...

Red Berry Bay

A family of choughs
k-chuffing,
lined up along their ledge.
One swoops, decides
to almost loop the loop,
red legs and beak against
jet black, against
the red of sandstone rock,
down to the deep
blue sea and rocky shore,
and up again to bright green
sloping meadows,
topped by pink thrift.

The seals are in
their tidal cave,
where black porphyry glistens
like their backs,
but here's one near us
riding on the waves,
those eyes, half-human,
gazing at us,
diving, reappearing
closer to us,
for minutes eyes locked
holding me transfixed.

The seagulls far off, floating
on the wind
like flecks of spume,
against the massive, sharp

striated rock,
deep red against the blue
of sky above and sea beneath.
And all across the bay
is held by God in play.

Sunset at Red Berry Bay

The sun, cold yellow, sinks
against a sky of shaded pinks,
into a calm, still sea
of turquoise blue.
Two pairs of choughs,
swift unexpected gift,
have come to celebrate,
ecstatic, acrobatic
in their display and interplay,
returning to their rocky ledge.
From the cliff edge we share,
in deep respect
and gathering delight,
the still mysterious dying
of the light.

Seals at Red Berry Bay

The earth is joyous
in the bright, unexpected
early autumn sun,
in the aftermath of storm
and endless rain.
The sea is playful,
lathered with froth and foam.
In the shelter of the bay,
two seals, frisky, kissing, coupling,
shiny black on grey,
disappearing, coming up for air,
held together in the gentle
rolling waves, that come gaily
breaking on the rocky shore.

The Old Barn

Ravens squatting in the gaps
between the broken ridge tiles,
grey stone collapsing
around the lintels,
everywhere the sweet smell
of rotted hay and of decay.
Tempted, wanting to explore,
I enter in the wide and open door,
past old and broken
farm machinery,
a vice that's rusted rigid
on the workbench,
rusty chains and tools
on hooks along the walls,
old hoists and pulley wheels,
on metal racks
a melded mass of screws.

And here and there
among the shadows,
rusted tool heads, an anvil,
pincers, blacksmith's hammer,
chisel, sickle,
wrench and spanner,
mattock, plough, and posthole spade,
two-handed saw, electric motor,
mains supply switch
rusted in the 'off' position.
Rats leaping as I tread
among the bins and empty sacks,
and running free along the rafters.
Dust motes floating
in a shaft of light—

relieved, I make my exit
into sunlight,
caught sight of
through a narrow door.

The Priory Pond

A bright blue sky
vivid with promise.
Sun and shadow
by the Priory pond,
on old stone walls
and overhanging trees,
bulrushes, water lilies,
violets and fleur-de-lis.
The surface mirrors
every shade of green:
duckweed, pondweed
arrowhead and buckbeam,
frogbit, mare's tail
and water horsetail.

Dragonflies, electric blue,
flashing in the early
summer light.
The pond skater
and the damselfly
dancing to
the hum of insects
in the rushes.
The water boatman,
on its boat-shaped back,
gracefully avoiding
the great diving beetle,
the whirligig gyrating,
the carp and stickleback.

Swallows skimming
criss-cross, open mouthed,
pied wagtails poking
on the margins,

mallard ducks and moorhens
with their trailing broods.
On the water's surface,
the glint of fin and tail.
The heron hidden, waiting
to disturb the peaceful calm.

Monastic Time

Nothing now to quieten
the dark wood
where memory abides,
or satisfy the soul's
deep longing,
but that daily meeting
God there in the real,
exposed to His
transforming gaze,
following along
the road of fire.

Passing time confronts
the geography of our past,
the spiritual distance,
and its landscape.
But time is now,
and every past encounter
served to change us;
blessings now surpass
memories that torment.
There is healing
in this interval
of waiting.

If once depths
of darkness shrouded
the anguish
and the sadness
of the past,
now seclusion's

sweet enchantment
fills the stillness
of this sacred ground,
like a small wood
dense with songbirds.

'My love...hiding in the clefts of the rock'

Gulls nesting
with their Easter young
in the clefts and hollows
of the limestone rock,
in the nooks and crannies,
in the deeper caves
below the Calvary above,
speaking of Christ's heart
pierced and broken, to provide
new life, a cleft
to nourish and protect.

We seek Christ's face,
and he desires
to see and hear us
where he dwells.
We feel his warmth,
we see his light,
deep down within
the dark cave of our heart.
From the deep heart
he pleads us
come back to him;
he calls us to enter in
to union with him.

Flying deeper, deeper,
drunk with love,
we seek to penetrate
the deepest recess,
to encounter there

his searing beauty,
to be hidden in
the mystery
of his open heart.

Hermit

Holy joy
and undomesticated
wildness.
Fierce, yet strangely
vulnerable
in your loving glance.
Who envies you
your solitude
and unrelenting silence,
praying for our
sin-scarred world?
A life nailed to the cross;
your God a living flame,
an all-consuming fire.

Islanders

Best if you can,
to be at peace
with God's plan,
and never, but never
rely on the weather.
Born to it
or called to it,
somehow chosen
or choosing,
not by head
but by heart,
to live out a life
by storm and by tide
from the world set apart.

Painting Lundy

Today, a Sunday,
begins as a grey day,
turns into a fun day,
when far away I see Lundy
from Caldey,
lit up by a sun's ray,
like a soufflé flambé.

Now, after days of storm,
contemplative calm's the norm,
until a noisy seagull
blocks my view,
and far away the ferry boat
goes out of frame
and it begins to rain.

No, not like Craigie Aitchison*
where all of life's profound,
the ordinary transfigured,
a perfect painted rhyme,
and all its colours glow and shine.

*Scottish Painter
1926—

On a Lazy Afternoon in Late Summer

Picture a cheeky robin
casually pulling a worm
from the ground
behind a cat
purring as it curls
its thin black tail
stretching its hot white paw
along the garden path
blinking at the sun blinking
behind the branches
of an apple tree
swaying in the breeze
dislodging an apple
startling the cat
startling the robin which
disappears into the tree
chased by the cat
until it drops the worm
on to the fallen apple
and flies off enraged
into the shade
to escape the cat
and the hot midday sun

Book Aid*

At least I'm saved
from languishing unread
in the darkest corner
of the bargain basement.
Freed from months in shrink-wrap,
I'm drawing breath
under African skies,
travelling to far off
exotic parts,
even if I'm wobbling
high up in a smelly crate,
exposed to flies and swatting tails,
desert heat and camel dung.
I'm participating in
the camel library
to nomads and refugees;
I'm here to nourish
those in need.
Even if I'm not remembered,
I'm bound to be well-thumbed
and I'll never, never, be remaindered.

*The Charity

Dewi Emrys*

Was he sad to die here?
Did his spirit soar?
High on a grassy cliff,
above a rocky shore,
memorial to a lover
of this place, Pwllderi.

Its simple splendour
neither salt wind
nor storm can mar.
Witness to a muse
still voyaging
on the eternal sea.

*David Emrys James
Poet, 1879-1952

Joan of Arc

Joan of Arc
at the stake
gave witness
to her faith.
The love of God
burned in her heart.
Heresy and witchcraft
were the charges;
but her courage came
from her famous 'voices',
accompanied
by brilliant light,
instructing her
to serve the Dauphin
and save France.
Fearless in battle,
at Orleans
she first donned her
shining armour white.
God's kingdom,
a voice within,
the spark
that set her life apart,
that led her in the field,
that caused her foes to yield.
The Holy Spirit's fire
consumed her on the pyre.

With Eager Longing....

With eager longing
we await
all that was lost, restored.
A time of grace
unbounded, a melody
so pure.
What seemed wild, untamed,
revealed as beauty,
revealing what is truest
deep within.
Recovering what was lost,
the landscape of innocence
we trod
when we were young.
Now free to live
that unlived life.

The Past is Another Country

The past is another country,
time closes the door.
Unable to go back, an aching gap
remains, an empty room
we cannot fill,
belonging to a time before.
It will not come again,
that unforgettable smile
eternally meant for us,
that look minutely remembered.
Something of the feeling roused
etched in the soul forever.
But we must move ever on,
haunted by the tragedy of living,
love still bearing
the unbearable weight of loss.
Was our longing then
too deep for this life?
Haunted from beyond,
our hearts are restless,
lacking hope, yet wanting
to be filled.
Not willing yet to risk,
not yet open to the new,
living uneasily in the present,
still endlessly longing.

The Past Transfigured

Eyes ocean deep,
caught out surveying
the archaeology of a past
we promised not to seek again,
now found hidden
among the new; sprung up
awkwardly aside the Hi-Tech
of our present lives, beneath
these barren trees and bitter skies,
those memories that cling,
refusing to be blotted out.
Like the waymark, stubborn
wildflowers, the date
on the weathered gravestone,
the tell-tale signs preserved
awakening our memories of loss—
of simple joys, regrets,
of love and tenderness,
the poetry between us—
finding a space in the soul,
a feeling in the heart, a longing
linking us to the time to come.
To trust in faith
that nothing finally is lost,
that all our past is held there,
free from all our failings, lack of love,
transfigured, waiting for us.

Pot-holing

Abseiling down
into the healing silence,
nothing but the distant
echo of a waterfall,
promising wild
unfathomed depths,
hidden chambers, mysteries
as yet uncovered.

Purer thought
opening up within.
Now all props gone,
groping for a foothold
in the dark,
on a journey without maps.
Brink of terror,
or breakthrough into
what was unknown and hidden,
discovery of the self within.

Healing darkness,
only faith to guide us.
Progressing without touch,
beginning now to learn
new climbing skills.
Stripping off the layers,
all illusion gone,
now living fully in the void.

Detached from all, and all
our false ideas of God,
now led by Him alone
into the unknown.
All is oneness,

standing here in truth
before the living God;
naked, resting
in not knowing.

Star-maker

'You will see heaven opened...'
John 1:51

What was there
before the cosmic dawn,
before the first young hot star
was born from cosmic fusion
and galaxies began to form and merge?
What was there before the beginning,
journeying backwards
through the telescope of time,
back in time around the Big Bang,
where the laws of physics break down?

Earth, improbable graveyard
of dead stars;
everything just right,
the elements combined
to bring forth life.
Debris from sacrificially
exploding stars
seeding the universe
with means of life.
Is there other life out there
near some faraway bright star?

Billions of stars
in one hundred billion galaxies,
what celestial skeleton
holds us all together
in this cosmic dance?
What is dark matter, what dark energy?
What is its mystery? Why?
What exists in unseen dimensions,

or through wormholes in space-time?
Will we see the heavens opened,
angels, God riding on the clouds,
another universe in parallel?
If all this wonder here exists,
what will be hereafter?

A Child in Time

As a child
He comes to us
is born in us
that His love in us
by His cross
set free
might grow in us
that His light
in us might show
that we in faith
and holiness
might grow
caught up in love
His Spirit know
His peace and joy
might flow

Simeon

Old man of deep
but firm desire, grown strong
from years of patient
yet expectant
waiting, ardent longing,
eager for the coming
of what lay as yet
unseen, so close but hidden
from all but those
with spiritual sight
and inner light.
The encounter, when it came,
was unexpected—
in a tiny child.
In-breath of love,
the holy man ecstatic,
joyful as he wrapped
his Saviour in his arms.
The Lord had come
into his temple
and filled his holy place
with his pure light.

Does Man Need a Suffering God?

Does man need
a suffering God?
Is sorrow really
part of love,
that infinite love
is seen to suffer so?—
sharing in
life's bitter sorrow,
hanging on a tree,
pouring love
as strong as fire
upon the world,
compelling
our response;
showing us
the door by which we enter,
the way that we must walk
into that other world,
our lives not crushed
but blessed,
carrying our neighbour
with his cross,
tenderly embracing all
who wronged us.

Crucifixion

Love made flesh.
His body
and His blood
become the pattern
of our offering.
He thirsts for our
loving will,
sets up His cross
within us,
as an altar
in our hearts,
for us to place
our obedient love
and free self-giving.

The Empty Tomb

The door that had seemed closed,
and firmly sealed,
has now been opened.
Christ has entered in,
has taken on himself, destroyed,
our deepest darkness.
No, there's nothing now
he cannot raise us up from,
if we but reach out,
if we will receive him.
That same power of love
that raised him
will raise us, free us
from all that holds us bound.
Now we're free
to choose to run
with eager love to meet him.
Now he has opened
the door that had seemed closed.

Easter Light

Enter in, surrender,
get caught up
within the action.
Let it come alive for you,
as participator, not spectator,
at the lighting
of the Easter fire;
when, placed at the cusp
where from the burning core
Christ soars into light,
you receive His life
and His embrace,
as He is placed on high.

If you have died with Him
then you will rise with Him,
freed from the inner darkness
that engulfs you and controls you,
all that drains and paralyses,
now freed for living His new life.
Living in Him,
carrying His new light,
by His transforming power
aware, alive enough to see
His life in each other—
even now His resurrection life.

Pentecost

'I came to cast down fire...'
Luke 12.49

You were fire, pure light
on the mountain top.
Your glory, epiphany,
lightning on the tree.
On the Cross all evil burned,
all creation quaked and shuddered.
Sacred mystery, Christ's blood shed
and body broken
on the mystic altar of the world,
and hallowing
the sacramental earth,
until the breakthrough
from the realms of death,
when He appeared in risen glory.

Your flame lit up the world
with your eternal fire
of love, transforming us
and all creation's tarnished beauty.
Your white heat, tongues of fire,
your Spirit setting all ablaze,
transforming hearts,
until our broken world
is whole again
and all creation taken up
into the cosmic Christ.

Jesus is Lord

All our freedom cannot overcome
what by sin we have become.
Only grace can heal us,
unlock God's power of love
to make within us
what was divided, one.

Christ our risen Lord alone,
by his Cross, can set us free
from all that binds us,
holds us back
from what we're called to be.

(song lyric)

Eucharist

I feel your gaze
of longing love,
eyes of fire
and pulsing light;
your presence thrills me,
fills me with delight.
In your quiet peace,
giving grace
you draw me to you;
and I, in awe
approach your otherness.
Your joy, your longing
to embrace,
fills all the space
between us.
Outside of self,
I know not how,
this time and place
no longer own me.

But you have more to give.
You long to come to me
in flesh and blood
and total love;
to fill, transform,
conform me
ever closer to you.
Our souls unite,
we touch, embrace,
you enter in
my deepest self;
joyful, deep communion

of delight,
enkindled by your
love and holy fire.
The Christ life living in me.

Humility

To truly live
in Christ, to share
his risen power,
to receive his gift,
to be filled to overflowing
with his love,
I must give myself away,
I must decrease,
he must increase in me.

Weak, relying
on his strength
working through me,
I must empty
to be filled
with his continuous
self-giving.
Joy shining
through the chaos,
sign of the world to come.

The Word

You come to me
in Sacrament and Word,
that your Word
may truly
live and grow,
become one flesh
with me,
unlocking depths,
loving others
through me.

Uncreated Light

In the stark
darkness
before dawn,
the icon candle
now extinguished,
yet a sweet
smell lingers.
A soft breeze sighs,
transports me
as if afar, yet present,
now beyond all sense,
sharing in the living God,
sharing in his love,
his goodness,
his pure joy and beauty.

The cell inside,
as if alight,
lights up the inner dark,
a dazzling dark
dissolved in light,
consuming fire
of grace, increasing
bright, pure deifying
uncreated light,
far brighter
than the sun,
vision of the things
to come.

Raids on the Unspeakable

Drawn into ever deeper darkness,
unfathomed silence, infinity of days,
into realms of the unspeakable,
that utter blackness, dense emptiness
where, there alone, the Word might speak
in utter purity and clarity,
his pure light pierce my blindness,
his fragrance burst upon my senses;
that I might draw breath from his pure essence,
that I might taste his sweetness,
he might touch me, breathe his spirit,
inflame my ardour with his love,
hold me rapt, if awe and terror
could give a face to Beauty.

The Beauty of the Word

Raw beauty he spoke,
that one creative Word
from which all being flowed.
The curtain rose,
the drama began,
the gift to be explored.
To seek to see with God's eyes
the revelation of his glory,
the beauty in all beauty,
the Spirit that gives life,
the face of the living Word
that we have heard;
bright Word, alive and active,
that captivates, attracts,
disturbs, repels,
dividing light from darkness.

Christ our light, transfigured beauty
of the Word who came
in flesh and blood
to live among us;
radiant, fragrant,
transforming beauty of his grace,
God-with-us,
holy, wholly other.
Face on which is written
the self-expression of
God's love for us,
how much he loves us,
up to death.
Beauty crucified
that saves, a love
that shares our pain,
that liberates and heals,

awakens faith,
brings back to life
all that's dead within.

That single simple Word, epiphany
of his goodness and his truth,
that does not pass away;
ever welling up
in joyful hearts renewed;
ever shaking to the core,
reshaping us in love.
Event that reveals
and acts, effects
his plan, his hidden fruitfulness
that does not return empty.
Sharp Word that judges and divides,
convicts, rejects
the ugliness of evil,
that banal corrupt seducer
of all that's good and true.
Hard Word of truth,
for some too hard to hear.
God's Word of life,
destined to be rejected
by some who cannot keep
its command to love with his love,
in order to be saved.

Keep the Fire Burning

Let the fire be kindled
in you, let the fire burn.
Yes, you can become all fire,
and all your desire
and darkness light.
Let it be kindled, let it grow
within you, let the Christ-life flow.
Give him your yes, become a light,
a flame, another Christ
for others, a light to light
their darkness, to catch
all souls on fire.
Let the Spirit's gift fan into flame
to spread the fire of Christ's love,
to find our peace there, to trust
in God alone.
So keep the fire ever burning,
hand on the sacred flame.

Morning Prayer

Praying, preparing the heart,
kindling love's fire;
desire, expectant longing,
for the light of truth.

Caught up in his Word,
by the open window,
waiting for the Son
to come.

Longing for Love and Union

In the interplay
of married lovers,
lost innocence
recovered.
Emptied, lifted out
of self, fulfilled,
becoming one
in one another.
Like to God
in loving union
and communion,
sign in this world
of God's love;
all our longing,
all our delight in giving,
all our love and joy,
is brought to birth
in giving life,
in reaching out
to others.
Like but unlike,
joined as one,
ecstatic, life-giving,
self-gift taken higher—
until our souls
break into fire.

Love Eros and Agape

A fierce and driven love impels us
out of self towards the other,
to be emptied to be filled,
made whole and deified,
to love all others with your love.
Following the path
of love you showed us,
the path you took to come to us,
the path you took to leave us,
our one desire to seek and see you.
You fill our souls with joyful longing,
with memories of ecstasy and wonder,
measureless delight.

Once dazzled by your beauty,
you take possession of our hearts,
preparing us for struggle,
for days of darkness
and your absence.
This is no human task you gave us.
We know but do not know the way.
Now dim the fire of love
and light of faith;
into the unknown you lead us,
following the unknowable,
naked in the dark.

Prayer

Breath of the soul,
natural as breath
the body breathes.
Slow in-breath
of Jesus,
slow out-breath
of the Spirit.
The body calm,
the spirit all intent.
No thought.
God as if seen—
but unseen—
below the threshold
of awareness.
God, his love, his will
replacing self.
Closer than breath,
indwelling.